Who Says You Can't Be

Perfect?

ALSO BY REVEREND AMBRIDGE

A Word of Hope
A Word of Hope—Revised Edition
Search the Word—Chapter One
The Path of Life

Who Says You Can't Be
Perfect?

As for God, his way is perfect; the word of the LORD is tried:
he is a buckler to all them that trust in him.
For who is God, save the LORD? and who is a rock, save our God?
God is my strength and power:
And he maketh my way perfect. 2 Samuel 22:31-33

Rev L. N. Ambridge

Library of Congress Control Number: 2011905502
ISBN: Softcover   978-1-4628-5311-3
                Ebook   978-1-4628-5312-0

All Scriptural references are from the Authorized King James Version of the Bible.

All translations from Greek and Hebrew are taken from the Exhaustive Concordance of the Bible, James Strong, S.T.D., LL.D., Hendrickson Publishers, Peabody, Massachusetts, United States.

All uses of the word "man" are anthropomorphic, from the Latin, meaning of human form. It refers to humankind as a whole, including both male and female, unless otherwise specified.

This book was printed in the United States of America.

To order additional copies of this book, contact:
Xlibris Corporation
1-888-795-4274
www.Xlibris.com
Orders@Xlibris.com
97633

Contents

PREFACE

Some people are what we call perfectionists. That means that no matter how well they do something, it's never good enough. Some parents have an attitude or a standard of perfection where their children are concerned. The child never seems to run fast enough or get high enough grades or dress well enough or do anything to the level of that parent's expectations. That can kill a person's confidence. At some point in your life you may have lost your confidence. Maybe you never had much. Perhaps someone told you something that shook your confidence in yourself. Or something happened that made you doubt your capabilities to do the things you wanted to or felt you should be able to do, because none of them could be done to the level of perfection that you thought you had to reach. Maybe you decided that you could do nothing more than just go with the flow, roll with the punches and just get by. Were you really happy? Were you satisfied?

Human beings have a sense of perfection, but it's not one that encourages hope or may even be reachable. That's not what God means by perfection.

There is a place we can reach in God, but the reaching of it is not within us. God can enable us and can do things in our lives that we could never do ourselves. He can empower us to do things we could never do through our own capacities. There is an abundant life, a life that Jesus talked about, that has its roots in the kingdom of God. It begins with the new birth and involves decisions that can put us in a place we've never been, a place where we function at our maximum potential in God. We can become more than conquerors.

What would you think if someone told you that you really can be perfect? What would happen if you believed that and decided to go for it?

What would happen if you made the decision to really live up to the command that Jesus issued, which is that we be perfect even as our Father which is in heaven is perfect? What if you could really do that and reap all the benefits of being the person God wants you to be? What if you didn't have to go through life missing the target and didn't have to look in the mirror at the end of the day and say wistfully, "Well, nobody's perfect"? What if you could look in the mirror at the end of the day and say something good happened? Something good like you made a decision to be what God wants you to be and honored that choice you made? Well, guess what? You can make that choice! And you can live by it, if you really want to, because God says you can! And if God says you can be perfect, who says you can't?

ACKNOWLEDGEMENTS

MY HEARTFELT APPRECIATION TO:

God, the Father, and Giver of everything that is good and perfect.

Jesus Christ, my Savior, who died that I may have the right to eternal life and peace.

The Holy Spirit, without whose inspiration I could never have written this book, and Who guides me through this world of darkness.

To all the people who have been a part of my life and made it a richer experience. To all the people who have believed in what God has called me to do and encouraged me to stay true to that calling.

I give my thanks.

DEDICATION

I dedicate this book to the One True God, to His precious Son, Jesus Christ, my Lord and Savior, and to the Holy Spirit without whose inspiration this book would never have been written.

INTRODUCTION

In a world where the word "perfect" means flawless, it can be unsettling to read in the Bible where Jesus commands us to be perfect.

The error lies in the interpretation of this command according to the modern English language instead of the ancient language in which the Scriptures were written. And it lies in our personal interpretation of what it means to be perfect. The fear comes from not understanding who God is and what He is likely to say and do. The fear comes from not knowing the God of love and glory. The fear comes from not realizing that God will never tell us to do something that is impossible, and that whatever He commands He will empower us and enable us to do.

God, in His infinite wisdom, knows that we must be renewed according to different standards than we used when we were strangers to His kingdom. The perfect that we know as unregenerate humanity is not the perfect that God commands. God is not talking so much about flaws. He's talking about commitment and application. Whatever flaws exist tend to be removed by applying the right standards.

This book is about understanding what God means when He commands perfection of His people. It is commanded; it is required, and it is possible through the power of the Holy Spirit! That's what He came for.

Do not think that God will love you less or reject you because there is work to be done in you. He looks on the heart and knows when we are sincere about our love and worship for Him. God knows the perfect heart.

It is my hope and prayer that, after you have read this book, you will understand what God wants from and for His people, and realize that everything God wants for us is necessary and good.

As we apply ourselves to reach the standard of perfection that God has set for us, we can only increase our knowledge of Him, improve our relationship with Him and increase our ability to walk this Christian way in wisdom and victory. That's what God wants for His people. That's the truth.

> Ye shall know the truth and the truth shall make you free.
> John 8:32

1

BE YE PERFECT

We are surrounded by perfection. Nature contains perfection in every imaginable form. Animals are perfectly adapted to their habitats. We can find perfect crystal formations in ice. Every snowflake has its own perfect pattern. Left to itself, each creature supports and promotes the life of something else in a perfect circle of nutrition. Grass eaters deposit fertilizer that promotes herbal growth. Grass eaters provide food for meat eaters. Meat eaters control the population. Carrion eaters clean the earth. Every form of life in the seas and oceans either controls population or provides food. Plants take in nitrogen and expel oxygen to provide a perfectly balanced atmosphere. When man does not interfere, everything is perfectly balanced. Everything is complete. Perfection is everywhere, except in humankind. We are off balance, out of sync, uncertain, inconsistent, inequitable, and so many other things. We intrude into the natural world and inevitably throw things out of rhythm. We are disproportionate to our environment and to each other and to God. We are imperfect.

I had never thought about God, but I did accept the fact that people are disproportionate to the environment and to each other. I examined my own life. I observed other people's lives. I studied history and the path that humanity had taken through the centuries. I tried to make myself believe that this was the way things had to be. Our humanness has forced us along this road of confusion, conflict and consternation. I used this to explain my faults and shortcomings and failures. My reasoning was that we just have to do the best we can with what we have, even though we don't seem to have very much. But it always seemed like there should be something more. It seemed like there should be a way to do this better. The version of truth I had manufactured for myself slipped through the holes of my reasoning like water through a fishnet. Somewhere deep inside there was a little corner of dissatisfaction I couldn't explain. The truth I tried to be comfortable with didn't really sound true. It didn't make me happy, nor did it provide satisfactory answers. And then, one day, I found out why . . .

PERFECTION ENCOUNTERED

One day, I met the ultimate truth. I came face to face with the One Absolute Truth that cannot be changed. He rose up in my life like a buoy that rises to the surface of the sea and bobs gently in the waves, not intrusive, not shouting, but always there, always undeniably, incontrovertibly, there. I tried to ignore Him. I tried to pretend He didn't exist. But He was always there, just at the edge of my vision, hovering on the horizon of my life, with open heart and outstretched arms.

I met the truth. I met peace. I met answers. I met perfection in the person of Jesus Christ. Life took on new meaning and depth. In the darkness of sin that surrounds us Jesus shines brighter than any beacon. The light that is shed by the Son of God not only shows us the imperfections in the human soul, but it shows us the way to overcome them. We are forced to drop all our defenses and excuses and the little lies we tell ourselves to try to make things okay. We face the reality of our sinfulness and imperfection and realize that He is the Way, the Truth, and the Life.

Sometimes people reject the reality and the ultimate consequence of sin. Maybe it hurts too much to face. Maybe it's too scary. Maybe people don't want to believe they don't have control. Maybe people are afraid God will kick them to the curb because of what they've done. Some people see God as they see other people. They see a God who will reject them because of their shortcomings, the way the world rejects them. But God is a God of mercy. As many as receive the truth receive the power to become the sons of God. We are raised from the deathbed of sin and born again of the water and the Spirit. We become the children of God. We discover that things we had thought were impossible are possible. We realize that the things of the Bible we saw as even foolish suddenly are wiser than anything we have ever known. The things we read about in the Bible are now potential realities for us. The righteousness we receive by faith opens the doors to opportunities in God and makes things possible. One of those unattainable things I discovered was that perfection is indeed not only possible, but required and necessary.

PERFECTION IS COMMANDED

We are required to walk in perfection because the Lord commanded it. Jesus said,

> Be ye therefore perfect, even as your Father which is in heaven is perfect. Matthew 5:48

I had tried to believe that humankind had to exist the way it was. But now, I met a divine command that contradicted the reasoning I had used to excuse myself. Jesus was telling me to do the very thing I had told myself could not be done. I had to admit, though, that if I had faith in God, then I had to agree that perfection must be possible, because God commands it. He will never direct us to do anything that is not possible through Him. He will never set a standard for us that we can't reach through Him. That's the key . . . through Him.

Jesus spoke the words, not as a request, but as a command. Do we have to comply? Read what Jesus said:

> If ye love me, keep my commandments. John 14:15

So, can I say I love Jesus, and not keep His commandments? There's another consideration.

> If ye keep my commandments, ye shall abide in my love; even as I have kept my Father's commandments, and abide in his love. John 15:10

There are many conditional statements in the Bible. The implication is that one condition presupposes another. In other words, when we say (or affirm) that we love the Lord, the logical result of that love is obedience to His commandments. If we love Jesus, then we keep His commandments. If we keep His commandments, then we abide in His love. If we abide in the love of Jesus, then we also abide in the love of the Father.

> For this is the love of God, that we keep his commandments: and his commandments are not grievous. 1 John 5:3

This is a critical point, because it's that divine love working through us that will make things possible. Jesus prefaced both His statements with the word "if." It means that people will say they love Him and still not obey Him. People will not always keep His commandments. Even people who have been born again of the water and the Spirit have the potential for disobedience, because they have a free will. It is a choice. Too many Christians still make the wrong choice. Too many call Him Lord, but don't treat Him as Lord.

> And why call ye me, Lord, Lord, and do not the things which I say? Whosoever cometh to me, and heareth my sayings, and doeth them, I will show you to whom he is like: He is like a man which built an house, and digged deep, and laid the foundation on a rock: and when the flood arose, the stream beat vehemently upon that house, and could not shake it: for it was founded upon a rock. But he that heareth, and doeth not, is like a man that without a foundation built an house upon the

earth; against which the stream did beat vehemently, and immediately it fell; and the ruin of that house was great. Luke 6:46-49

Read this passage and understand that the Lord commands things of us that are for our own good. When He commands something of us, it's because He knows it will help us. I can testify to this: every time I have disobeyed God (and I knew it was God speaking) I have found myself in a terrible mess. I could have avoided that mess by obeying His voice. God does not command arbitrarily; He commands for our preservation and victory. Those things God tells us to do will keep us on the path to glory.

PERFECTION BY MAN'S DEFINITION

Some people say that Jesus didn't mean perfect in the literal sense; He really meant mature. How can this make sense? What is it about the command to be perfect that makes it unacceptable to the human mind?

Maybe people don't believe in perfection because they assume Jesus was referring to the modern day definition of perfect that says we can't have any faults or defects or flaws. How do people reconcile Jesus' command with their finite view of perfection? They change the command! They give it a definition that is comfortable and reachable. But then . . . if you lower the standard you not only create a new standard, but you also miss the requirement that was originally established! So you still have not obeyed God, but your own interpretation!

When we change the requirement we create a new standard. We quote Jesus this way, "Be ye therefore mature, even as your Father which is in heaven is mature."

We have not only changed the Word of God; we have also changed our perception of the nature of God. The reality is this:

1. Who is to say what "mature" means in relation to God?
2. How do we know when we have reached maturity?
3. If God is mature, when was He immature? The Bible says He is the same yesterday, today, and forever.
4. How shall we judge the maturity of God?

> Nay but, O man, who art thou that repliest against God? Shall the thing formed say to him that formed it, Why hast thou made me thus? Romans 9:20

To reach maturity one must begin in some state of immaturity. When was God immature? When did He change? How did He change? How long did it take Him to reach maturity? What was He like then compared to what He's like now? At what point could God be considered to have reached maturity? The answer is this. There was no change. There was no beginning and there is no end. There was no process where God is concerned.

> Jesus said unto them, verily, verily, I say unto you, Before Abraham was, I am. John 8:58

> Jesus Christ the same yesterday, and today, and forever. Hebrews 13:8

> Every good gift and every perfect gift is from above, and cometh down from the Father of lights, with whom is no variableness, neither shadow of turning. James 1:17

These are only a few of the many Scriptures that confirm to us that God is the same now as He was in the beginning and will be forevermore. The description of maturity suggests that there is a need for development. We can draw the conclusion, therefore, that God cannot be judged as mature, because He was never immature. He never had to change or adapt to become what and who he is now. God is.

We as human beings do grow and mature. But the Scripture doesn't say mature; it says perfect. And we know that God is perfect, because He is complete within Himself. There is nothing more needed to make Him what He is.

By the very nature of the word "mature" we say that God began as immature and had to grow up to be as He is now. The word "mature" means to achieve a certain level of development through a growth process. The implication is that once I reach a certain level of development, I will be at the same level as God. That leads to the premise that, if I can be at the same level as God, I can be God. Ergo, I do not need God. I just need to reach the right stage of development. This is dangerous thinking.

Eve made the same mistake, although she tried to take a shortcut by eating the forbidden fruit. She let the temptation of becoming a super power lead her to her death.

Sometimes I think the infatuation with Wonder Woman and Superman and all the other superheroes reflects a desire to be superhuman. Humans seem to have this deep down wish to be a super power, to have super human abilities that allow us to rise above all circumstances and become the ultimate conqueror. That's actually understandable considering the fact that we live in a world that daily threatens to overwhelm and defeat us.

It's understandable, but not acceptable. We are not super powers. We do not have super human abilities. The super hero sagas are fun and entertaining, but they're not real. We cannot be God, but we can be such that we reflect His glory, like the moon reflects the light of the sun. We can be such that we can depend on God to keep us through the storms that threaten to sink our boat. God is and always has been perfect.

He is the same yesterday, today, and forever.

PERFECTION BY GOD'S DEFINITION

> Be ye perfect, even as your Father, which is in heaven, is perfect. Matthew 5:48

This passage contains the word "perfect" as translated from the Greek "teleios." This word has several different meanings according to Strong's Exhaustive Concordance of the Greek:

1. Of full age
2. Brought to its end
3. Finished

4. Wanting nothing necessary to completeness
5. Consummate human integrity and virtue
6. Adult
7. Mature

It's important to examine the content of a statement in order to understand the full meaning. Jesus gave us the required measurement (perfect) and He also gave us the yardstick against which we are to measure ourselves (the Father in heaven). Let's compare our list of definitions against the yardstick.

1. Of full age—God is not of full age because He was never young.
2. Brought to its end—God has no end.
3. Finished—God will never be finished. He is still very active and will always be. And he is not in a state of development.
4. Wanting nothing necessary to completeness—Think about this one.
5. Consummate human integrity and virtue—God is certainly above human integrity and virtue!
6. God is not an adult because He was never a child.
7. Mature—We have already confirmed that mature is not included in the definition of perfect where God is concerned.

There is only one definition in this list that fits the requirement—wanting nothing necessary to completeness. Therefore we establish that the meaning of the command is this: Having been born again as children of God, we are to add those things (or allow God to add them to us) that bring us to a state of completeness where we lack nothing in order to be considered sons of God.

In Jesus' time, a son was supposed to be the reflection of his father. He was supposed to perform his father's will and personify his father's attributes and principles and practices. When he did so, he was as his father.

PERFECTION IS POSSIBLE

We have already received the condition of perfection by proxy. We stand under the covering of Jesus Christ. We are declared judicially perfect, as if we had never sinned. We are positionally perfect, because we are reconciled back to God. The foundation of perfection has been laid. Now we have to build on it. The capability is there and the potential is there, through Jesus. When we are able to be perfect as Jesus commanded, then we will be as our Father in heaven, not replacing Him or competing with Him, but simply reflecting Him so that the world will know we are His children. That's what the Scripture means in the first chapter of John's Gospel:

> But as many as received him, to them gave he power to become the sons of God, even to them that believe on his name: Which were born, not of blood, nor of the will of the flesh, nor of the will of man, but of God. John 1:12-13

Because we have believed on His Name, He has given us the power to become the sons of God. We have been given the power, through faith, to obey every command Jesus spoke. We have been given the power to be perfect even as our Father, which is in heaven, is perfect. It is not by our definition or our devices, but by His definition, and by His power that we can be what He wants us to be!

WHO IS RESPONSIBLE FOR PERFECTION?

THE MINISTRY RESPONSIBILITY

God has anointed certain people and placed them in the church with the responsibility of helping the saints to become equipped so that they may become complete (perfect) in Christ. This was Paul's testimony and it is true of everyone that is called to labor in the ministry.

> Whereof I am made a minister, according to the dispensation of God which is given to me for you, to fulfil the word of God; Even the mystery which hath been hid from ages and from generations, but now is made manifest to his saints: To whom God would make known what is the riches of the glory of this mystery among the Gentiles; which is Christ in you, the hope of glory: Whom we preach, warning every man, and teaching every man in all wisdom; that we may present every man perfect (teleios—complete) in Christ Jesus: Whereunto I also labour, striving according to his working, which worketh in me mightily. Colossians 1:25-29

Not everyone is called or anointed to equip the saints. This is a new thing that has developed in the modern church—the belief that everyone is called and everyone is anointed and everyone is designated for ministry. The ministry will prove itself, because the anointing will come forth. It will be evident and unmistakable, under close, prayerful scrutiny and comparison against the Word.

> And he gave some, apostles; and some, prophets; and some, evangelists; and some, pastors and teachers; For the perfecting (katartismos—complete furnishing) of the saints, for the work of the ministry, for the edifying of the body of Christ: Till we all come in the unity of the faith, and of the knowledge of the Son of God, unto a perfect (teleios—complete) man, unto the measure of the stature of the fulness of Christ: That we henceforth be no more children, tossed to and fro, and carried about with every wind of doctrine, by the sleight of men, and cunning craftiness, whereby they lie in wait to deceive; But speaking the truth in love, may grow up into him in all things, which is the head, even Christ: From whom the whole body fitly joined together and compacted by that which every joint supplieth, according to the effectual working in the measure of every part, maketh increase of the body unto the edifying of itself in love. Ephesians 4:11-16

The important thing to remember and apply is that the Word of God is the final authority. No one teaching or preaching contrary to the Word of God can be accepted as serving God.

THE SAINTS' RESPONSIBILITY

We are not to leave everything in the hands of the ministry. The saints must meet the ministry half way and make an effort to receive and apply what is taught and preached. In the Book of Philippians the Apostle Paul urged the saints to continue in their pursuit of perfection in the Lord. He warned them not to assume that they had everything they needed in Jesus.

> Not as though I had already attained, either were already perfect: but I follow after, if that I may apprehend that for which also I am apprehended of Christ Jesus. Brethren, I count not myself to have apprehended: but this one thing I do, forgetting those things which are behind, and reaching forth unto those things which are before, I press toward the mark for the prize of the high calling of God in Christ Jesus. Let us therefore, as many as be perfect, be thus minded: and if in anything ye be otherwise minded, God shall reveal even this unto you. Philippians 3:12-15

Paul reminded the congregation at Philippi that he did not assume he had reached perfection and neither should they. This is the responsibility of every Christian. Even when we think we are complete (perfect) in God, we should continue to compare ourselves against the Word of God to make sure we haven't left anything lacking. This is important, because the moment we think we have everything we need, we stop trying.

There is a conversation between Jesus and a rich young ruler recorded in the Gospel of Matthew, Chapter 19:16-24. We could glean a lot from this passage, but our focus right now is on the pursuit of perfection (completeness in God).

This young man had a question for the Lord: "What good thing shall I do, that I may have eternal life?" Jesus told him to keep the commandments. The young man asked, "Which?" Jesus responded as follows:

- Thou shalt do no murder.
- Thou shalt not commit adultery.
- Thou shalt not bear false witness.
- Honor thy father and mother.
- Thou shalt love thy neighbor as thyself.

The last commandment corresponds to the Old Testament commandment that says we are not to covet anything that belongs to one's neighbor. That is the outworking of love of one's neighbor. We shouldn't get so caught up in wanting what others have that it threatens our relationship.

It is significant that Jesus quoted the last six commandments to the young man, but not the first four. The last six pertain to the relationships between human beings. The young man was concerned with attaining eternal life; apparently he already was committed to God in regard to the first four Commandments, which address the relationship with God and humanity.

Otherwise, I believe the Lord would have quoted all Ten Commandments. Jesus knew that the young man did lack something in his relationships with people. He was incomplete in his faith. Can we love God without also loving our fellow human beings?

Here comes the key question.

> The young man saith unto him All these things have I kept from my youth up. What lack I yet? Matthew 19:20

In response to the young man's question about lacking, Jesus answered

> If thou wilt be perfect, go and sell all that thou hast, and give to the poor, and thou shalt have treasure in heaven and come and follow me. Matthew 19:21

Jesus responded to a concern about incompleteness with a solution for completeness. The Lord's command to sell everything was a gauge as well as a revelation of the ruler's degree of commitment to God and equipping in God. We have a hard time being committed to God without the right equipment to work with. Look at what happened. The young man "went away sorrowful; for he had great possessions."

The young ruler was committed to God, but his heart was not perfect (complete) toward God in his commitment. There was a part of him that he could not give up. Does this mean that we are not perfect in our commitment to God if we don't sell everything and give to the poor? No it does not! Will God tell us to sell everything we have and give it to the poor? Maybe He will; maybe He won't. That depends on who you are and what God has called you to be.

That's not the point. The point is this: perfection means being completely committed to God so that we are prepared to do whatever He tells us to do. Perfection means having everything we need in Christ so that we are not found lacking when God approaches and examines.

WHAT LACK I YET?

What do we lack in reaching that goal of perfection? We find out by looking in the mirror and doing a close examination. Our mirror is the Word of God. When we measure ourselves against that divine measuring rod, it's easy to see the shortage. That means we need to study.

> Study to show thyself approved unto God, a workman that needeth not to be ashamed, rightly dividing the word of truth. 2 Timothy 2:15

VERY, VERY, IMPORTANT: It's not only the studying by which we show ourselves approved unto God; it's also the application. We study to find out what to apply; then we apply it. We can't show ourselves approved to God unless we know what it takes. That comes with study. Paul told Timothy to keep living what he had learned.

> But continue thou in the things which thou hast learned and hast been assured of, knowing of whom thou hast learned them; 2 Timothy 3:14

It does no good to study the Bible if we don't apply what we learn. That's the only way we learn to use the equipment we get from prayer and study. The Word of God is a sword to divide the natural man from the spiritual man, but if we never use it, there is no separation and no growth. It's not just by living a moral life that we maintain our salvation, but by living a holy life according to the Word and will of God.

All scripture is given by inspiration of God, and is profitable for doctrine, for reproof, for correction, for instruction in righteousness: That the man of God may be perfect (artios—meaning fitted, complete), thoroughly furnished unto all good works. 2 Timothy 3:16-17

We mess things up sometimes. We disappoint the Father some days. But if we concentrate our energies on perfecting our hearts through obedience to the Word the disappointments will come less and less frequently. A heart that is perfect before God and is equipped and furnished with what it needs to reach the fullness of the measure of Christ will shape the character. A mind that is equipped and renewed in holiness will govern the thoughts in the way of life.

So . . . . take whatever equipment you find for yourself and whatever equipment you receive from the ministry and use it all. The ministry people will even show you how to use it if you need assistance. But remember, God means for you to be equipped in order to be brought to perfection. (Ambridge 2011)

If God provides you with the proper equipment, who says you can't be perfect?

2

THE FIRST FOUR RULES

Be ye therefore perfect, even as your Father which is in heaven is perfect. Matthew 5:48 KJV

"Nobody is perfect but Jesus and I'm not Him!" How many times have you heard that statement? Yet Jesus commanded us to be just that . . . . perfect. We say we believe that the Bible is the inspired word of God, yet we don't hesitate to change it when the situation suits us. What is it about the command to be perfect that makes it unacceptable to the human mind?

Perhaps people don't believe in perfection because they assume Jesus was referring to the classic definition of perfect which is "to be entirely without fault or defect." How does one do that while still encased in these clay vessels? One doesn't, not without help and guidance and the power of the Holy Spirit.

Let's examine the words that immediately preceded the command.

> Ye have heard that it hath been said, Thou shalt love thy neighbour, and hate thine enemy. But I say unto you, Love your enemies, bless them that curse you, do good to them that hate you, and pray for them which despitefully use you, and persecute you; That ye may be the children of your Father which is in heaven: for he maketh his sun to rise on the evil and on the good, and sendeth rain on the just and on the unjust. For if ye love them which love you, what reward have ye? do not even the publicans the same? And if ye salute your brethren only, what do ye more than others? do not even the publicans so? Matthew 5:43-47

Jesus preceded the command to perfection with four other commands:

> Love your enemies
> Bless them that curse you
> Do good to them that hate you
> Pray for them which despitefully use you and persecute you

Love your enemies. Why would God want you to love your enemies? Why should you love someone who is interested only in despising and disrespecting you? But then, why did God love you when you were His enemy?

> But God commendeth his love toward us, in that, while we were yet sinners, Christ died for us. Much more then, being now justified by his blood, we shall be saved from

wrath through him. For if, when we were enemies, we
were reconciled to God by the death of his Son, much
more, being reconciled, we shall be saved by his life.
Romans 5:8-10

The answer lies in the word "love." The love that God has for
humanity is not the emotional, self-centered love that we show
for one another. The worldly level of love is the kind that loves
on condition, depending on whether the object "deserves" to
be loved. It's a form of love that makes the giver feel good
about giving, depending on the "goodness" or merit of the one
being loved. It needs outside reinforcement. The love of God
runs under its own power, because love is who He is and what
He is about. The kind of love God embodies is altruistic. That
means it's a giving love. It does whatever is good and right for
the one that is loved. It gives whether it receives or not. That's
the love of God.

Being born again of the water and the Spirit means that the
Spirit of God comes to abide with us. That means He guides us
and inspires us from day to day. If that is so, then it follows that
we are guided by His character. That's what the Bible says.

> And hope maketh not ashamed; because the love of God
> is shed abroad in our hearts by the Holy Ghost which is
> given unto us. Romans 5:5

> Beloved, let us love one another: for love is of God; and
> every one that loveth is born of God, and knoweth God.
> He that loveth not knoweth not God; for God is love. In
> this was manifested the love of God toward us, because

that God sent his only begotten Son into the world, that we might live through him. Herein is love, not that we loved God, but that he loved us, and sent his Son to be the propitiation for our sins. Beloved, if God so loved us, we ought also to love one another. No man hath seen God at any time. If we love one another, God dwelleth in us, and his love is perfected in us. Hereby know we that we dwell in him, and he in us, because he hath given us of his Spirit. 1 John 4:7-13

Being able to love with the love of God is a validation of our relationship with Him. We know we dwell in Him if His love is active in us toward Him and in turn toward others. When we can love others with the love of God, His love is "perfected" in us. It is complete in its application according to His will and His character. As He loves, so we love.

The result of obedience is this: "that ye may be the children of your Father which is in heaven." Another meaning for perfect is something that is an exact replica of the original. Jesus, as He spoke these commands, used the Father as our reference point, our original model. He causes the sun to rise on the evil and on the good, and sends rain on the just and the unjust.

God is love, the agape, giving, altruistic love that operates, not by selfish, egocentric emotion, but by the principle of acting for the good of all. When we can get to the point where we operate the way God operates, we will be replicating Him and therefore His perfection. In other words, the command to be perfect forms a parenthesis in which are contained the four preceding commands to love, bless, do good and pray. Obedience to the first four requirements precedes obedience to the fifth and ultimate requirement.

Can you let God help you love your enemies? Can you let God take you to the point where you can bless them that curse you? Can you do good to them that hate you as God has done good for you? Can you purify your heart through obedience to the Word so that you can pray for them which despitefully use you and persecute you?

If you decided to get to the place where you can let God do this work in you, then you have decided on perfection (completeness). If God says you can, who says you can't?

3

THE PERFECTION OF PURPOSE

Jesus emphasized several characteristics we need to exhibit in order to reach the level on which God has always operated. There is no subjectivity. The Bible is very clear on these measurable, observable traits of character.

The word translated means "complete" and refers to the level of application. How fully do you function according to the aspects of your existence? How completely do you apply yourself to the reason for which you are? There is a term in the French language; raison d'être, the reason for existing.

We know that God is love. We know that He is omniscient, omnipotent, omnipresent and eternal. Does He fulfill all these aspects on a daily basis? Yes, He does! In Him is complete application of all aspects of His existence.

Let's step back to Genesis for a moment. God set out with a purpose in mind. He created the heavens, the earth, the seas, land, and sentient creatures. On the sixth day he created man, in His own image. This was not an afterthought. Consider the following Scriptures:

> Then shall the King say unto them on his right hand, Come, ye blessed of my Father, inherit the kingdom prepared for you from the foundation of the world: Matthew 25:34 KJV

> Blessed be the God and Father of our Lord Jesus Christ, who hath blessed us with all spiritual blessings in heavenly places in Christ: According as he hath chosen us in him before the foundation of the world, that we should be holy and without blame before him in love: Having predestinated us unto the adoption of children by Jesus Christ to himself, according to the good pleasure of his will, To the praise of the glory of his grace, wherein he hath made us accepted in the beloved. Ephesians 1:3-6 KJV

> For we which have believed do enter into rest, as he said, As I have sworn in my wrath, if they shall enter into my rest: although the works were finished from the foundation of the world. Hebrews 4:3 KJV

> Forasmuch as ye know that ye were not redeemed with corruptible things, as silver and gold, from your vain conversation received by tradition from your fathers; But with the precious blood of Christ, as of a lamb without blemish and without spot: Who verily was foreordained before the foundation of the world, but

was manifest in these last times for you, Who by him
do believe in God, that raised him up from the dead,
and gave him glory; that your faith and hope might be
in God. 1 Peter 1:18-21 KJV

What phrase do you see repeated? It is "the foundation of the
world." Study these Scriptures. The thought that will become
clear to you is this: God did not create man for the world. He
created the world to reflect his glory! And He created man as a
reflection of Himself, to take care of that world! As man cares for
the world that was to reflect the glory of God, man himself takes
part in that reflection. Now we know that Satan ruined everything
by his maneuvering Adam and Eve into sin and that the world is
now under a curse. So what's left to reflect the glory of God but
humankind? But we can't do that in a sinful state. God had us in
mind and created a place for us to be. He made the world and gave
it to us to care for. Do you feel special yet? Do you feel loved? Do
you feel accountable? Do you see that it is your responsibility as
a Christian to try to be who God created you to be? He is here to
help, so it's not as if perfection were impossible.

When God had finished His creative project, He rested. He
had completely fulfilled His purpose for that time and place
and completely applied every aspect of His character. That's
one example to us of the perfection of God. He functions
according to Who He is and why He exists. He lacks nothing in
the application of His character; His use of His capabilities is
complete in everything He does.

What about you? Why do you exist? For what purpose did
God create you? Do you function according to who you are?

Our common purpose is to exist to the praise of His glory. That means we glorify God in our lives, in all we think, say and do. Because we each are unique persons, we each have a unique way of glorifying the Father, but it all has the same foundation.

Now we could argue the point that people who are not saved but are complete in their application of wickedness are perfect because they function according to who they are. But God did not create man to be wicked.

> And God said, Let us make man in our image, after our likeness: and let them have dominion over the fish of the sea, and over the fowl of the air, and over the cattle, and over all the earth, and over every creeping thing that creepeth upon the earth. So God created man in his own image, in the image of God created he him; male and female created he them. And God blessed them, and God said unto them, Be fruitful, and multiply, and replenish the earth, and subdue it: and have dominion over the fish of the sea, and over the fowl of the air, and over every living thing that moveth upon the earth.

> And God said, Behold, I have given you every herb bearing seed, which is upon the face of all the earth, and every tree, in the which is the fruit of a tree yielding seed; to you it shall be for meat. And to every beast of the earth, and to every fowl of the air, and to every thing that creepeth upon the earth, wherein there is life, I have given every green herb for meat: and it was so.

> And God saw every thing that he had made, and, behold, it was very good. And the evening and the morning were the sixth day. Genesis 1:26-31

Perfection is when we completely fulfill God's purpose for our lives. Therefore, the unsaved can never reach perfection because that wasn't mankind's purpose. That wasn't why man was created. God did not create man to live a sinful life. God created man in His own image. That means man was meant to reflect the glory of God on earth. Sin was the work of Satan who brought about the fall of the human race by leading the first man and woman into rebellion against God's law. Humankind was cast into the darkness of sin and separation from God.

We are supposed to function according to the character of holiness that exists in God and that becomes active in us once we have been born again of the water and the Spirit. When we are born again of the water and the Spirit, it returns us to our original state of sinlessness, as when God first created humankind. Adam and Eve were perfect in God. Even Satan was perfect in his beauty, until he became corrupted by his own pride.

When we reach the point where we apply ourselves fully and completely according to the Spirit of Holiness who dwells in us and according to the character of the Holy God who created us, and in line with the reason for which we were created, fulfilling the purpose for which we were created; that is perfection according to the will of God! This does not make us God but makes us complete in God.

Are you determined to have the Father's will consummate in your life? Are you committed to push through to perfection and the complete working out of God's purpose for you? Can you do that? Can you be complete in your commitment and obedience to the will of God for your life? Can you be everything God wants you to be and do everything God wants you to do and finish the work He has given you for your life (knowing that He will empower and enable you to do so)? Can you be perfect? Who says you can't do that when God says you can?

4

THE RELATIVITY OF PERFECTION

The word "relativity" means that something exists in relation to something else. Salvation is universal. It is the same for everyone. The requirements are the same; the end result is the same. Perfection is universal and at the same time relative. It exists overall in relation to God and it exists uniquely in each person God has created. God created us in His own image. That means we have rational thought. We have a free will. We can make decisions. We have emotions. We can plan and imagine and analyze and meditate. We can remember the past and speculate about the future. We can entertain hope about things to come. And we can harbor faith.

We have one common design and purpose—to live to the praise of His glory. But there is one thing about each of us that is unique. That is the individual personality. That never changes. When we are born again in Christ, we are born again as a new creature, indwelt with the Holy Spirit. But He does not replace our personality. Rather He makes it possible for us to behave with a new character, a new imprint. The old character of sin is neutralized and the new character of holiness is brought forth within us.

> Therefore if any man be in Christ, he is a new creature: old things are passed away; behold, all things are become new. 2 Corinthians 5:17

We use the passage in 2 Corinthians 5:17 all the time to define our new life in Christ. This passage does not mean we acquire a different personality; that we become someone else. Do not make the mistake of thinking you have to BE someone else in order to be saved. Do not think you have to be the pastor or the preacher or a carbon copy of some other saint in the church. You don't have their personality, so you can't be them. But you can follow their example of godliness.

You are not a carbon copy of anyone else. You don't have their personality. You have your own personality. You serve God best as yourself, not as trying to be someone else! That's why the perfection in God that each of us achieves is relative to the person God made us to be.

When the Scripture speaks of things that are passed away and things that are become new, it's referring to the character. Our personality is who we are. It will not change. But our character is the person we display, the way we live, the way we address issues in life. That can change and it does change as we go through life and through seasons and experiences. When we are born again in Christ, our character undergoes a major change, because we don't display ourselves the way we used to, as children of wrath and products of the natural mind, the world, the flesh, and the devil. We begin to address issues a different way. We acquire a new perspective. We approach life differently.

So, that being said, how does our character change? Consider the following passage:

> Whereby are given unto us exceeding great and precious promises: that by these ye might be partakers of the divine nature, having escaped the corruption that is in the world through lust. And beside this, giving all diligence, add to your faith virtue; and to virtue knowledge; And to knowledge temperance; and to temperance patience; and to patience godliness; And to godliness brotherly kindness; and to brotherly kindness charity. 2 Peter 1:4-6

Realize that we must take the foundation of faith that God has given and we begin to build on it. Don't even think you can reach perfection in God without first being in God!

We go to Sunday school and Bible Study and worship service to hear the revelation of the Word that God gives to His anointed to pass on to us. We search and study the Scriptures and confirm for ourselves what we have heard. We meditate on these things. We apply what we learn to the basic personality God has given each one of us. We add those things that God will use to reshape our character: virtue, knowledge, temperance, patience, godliness, brotherly kindness, charity and so forth. Realize that these are attributes of character. They are the personality of God that we apply to reshape our character so that we may behave as children of God.

Many people will respond to the requirement of the Scripture by saying, "Nobody is perfect. I'm not perfect." But in this case perfection is a relative term. Individual saints must strive for perfection by becoming all that God desires in each of their lives. We must focus our efforts on acquiring the character that enables us to function the way God meant us to function. When we reach the point where we are living godly lives and fulfilling the purpose that God intends for each one of us, we will have reached perfection as God wills it for each of us. What is your purpose? God will reveal it in time. Paul said it well to the saints at Corinth who were trying to be everything at once.

> For as the body is one, and hath many members, and all the members of that one body, being many, are one body: so also is Christ. For by one Spirit are we all baptized into one body, whether we be Jews or Gentiles, whether we be bond or free; and have been all made to drink into one Spirit. For the body is not one member, but many. If the foot shall say, Because I am not the hand, I am not of the body; is it therefore not of the body? And if the ear shall say, Because I am not the eye, I am not of the body; is it therefore not of the body? If the whole body were an eye, where were the hearing? If the whole were hearing, where were the smelling? But now hath God set the members every one of them in the body, as it hath pleased him. And if they were all one member, where were the body? But now are they many members, yet but one body. 1 Corinthians 12:12-20

No one person can do everything. No one person can reach everybody in the gospel. Every personality is unique and every person has a unique place in the body of Christ. Just as the pieces of a jigsaw puzzle are uniquely shaped, each unique personality joins with the others to form a complete unit.

> Finally, brethren, farewell. Be perfect, be of good comfort, be of one mind, live in peace; and the God of love and peace shall be with you. 2 Corinthians 13:11

In Paul's farewell to the church at Corinth, he urged them to be "perfect." The word translated here is "katartizo," which means to be perfectly joined, to fit together. Paul was making a plea for unity, that the brethren, though each of them was different, should join together seamlessly in Christ, each one fulfilling his separate role, but each one fitting in with the other, one taking up the slack where another fell short. Paul's encouragement for perfection echoes the commission recorded in Ephesians 4:16, that the "whole body be fitly joined and compacted by that which every joint supplieth." Every faithful member adds something to the working of the body, the church.

Here's a very simple test for relative perfection. Try to eat clear soup with a fork. What happens? The broth escapes through the tines of the fork and you get nothing but a small trace of flavor. Now use a spoon. You get all the broth without spilling it or losing it. In considering the best way to eat soup, a fork is not appropriate because it was not designed for eating soup. Therefore, a fork can never fulfill its purpose and will never be perfect. A spoon is designed to catch up liquids and is the perfect instrument for eating soup. The spoon is fulfilling the purpose for which it was designed. The spoon is perfect for eating soup. You get the full flavor, the full effect, and the full benefit.

We all have a basic purpose to be saved, and in living the saved life, to glorify God in each of our lives. But if, in addition to that purpose, I try to reach perfection by becoming a copy of another person, I become that fork, and all the liquid escapes. I could try to walk in someone else's shoes; and try to do what God has determined for someone else to do, but the result would be only mediocre. It would never reach the standard that God had designed.

I don't achieve perfection. I don't achieve anything but desperation and a sense of failure because I can't preach that sermon or run that revival or even perhaps pray that powerful prayer I heard on Sunday, or bake that marvelous pie for the church supper or make those pews glisten with wax or be johnny-on-the-spot and have a knack for anticipating every need as the Pastor's Aide.

Maybe I'm not a great mechanic that keeps the church van purring or maybe I can't interact with the teenagers in the youth Sunday School, or be a whiz at balancing the church financial books, but when I focus on becoming the person God designed me to be (whatever that is), when I apply my efforts to fit myself into the Scripture and obey His Word for my life, I approach perfection because I am approaching the pattern God has established for my life. It's not wise to compare myself with anyone else, because I am not anyone else. I am the person God has created me to be. I achieve maximum effectiveness in God by being myself in Christ.

> For we dare not make ourselves of the number, or compare ourselves with some that commend themselves: but they measuring themselves by themselves, and comparing themselves among themselves, are not wise. 2 Corinthians 5:12

I may not have the knack of running the church nursery in such a way that it keeps all those tiny little people organized and happy. But perhaps I'm one of the saints of God to whom people are drawn, that they find easy to talk to and find comfort in my company. Or it could be that I'm one of those saints to whom God always gives a word of comfort and encouragement for someone. Perhaps my home is one where my children's friends like to gather and stay off the streets and out of trouble, because they find a special warmth in being there.

The ways that God works through people are as many and as varied as God's people themselves. However God shapes your life and your way, whatever He gives you to do, do it perfectly, with a complete and total commitment.

If you must compare yourself with someone, compare yourself with the Scripture. Compare yourself with the requirements God has set. If you want to know who you are in Christ, find out who God is. He knows you and can tell you who you are. Use the Bible for a mirror and God will show you yourself.

Remember that the anointed people in the five point ministry (apostles, prophets, evangelists, pastors, and teachers) are not better than you or more saved than you. They are just designated for a special responsiblity.

Where do we begin? Jesus told us:

> Be ye therefore perfect, even as your Father which is in
> heaven is perfect. Matthew 5:48 (KJV)

Don't take this passage out of context. Jesus gave us a starting
point for achieving perfection. Go back to Matthew 5:21 and
read to the end of the chapter. Then work your way through
the rest of God's Word. Apply what you learn as you learn it.
It works! It's good to have an example in the church to follow,
but don't lose yourself in trying to be who they are. It's good
to follow them that are following Christ. Use that example of
dedication and virtue and holiness. Imitate their character (the
Bible calls it conversation, behavior) but maintain your identity
in the Lord.

Consider this illustration.

The school system does not teach handwriting any more (sadly).
But there was a time when each student had to learn the Palmer
method of handwriting, to ensure that their handwriting was
legible and neat. Students had to practice forming letters
and words and they did writing exercises to develop proper
penmenship. All the students learned to form the same letters
the same way. It was a universal, common style of penmanship.
But once they had passed through the handwriting exercises and
learned to write, students were released from the writing class
to go on to other endeavors. Eventually, they began to develop
their own unique styles of handwriting, based on their individual
personalities and characters.

The universal foundation of salvation is the same for every person who comes to Christ. The rules are the same; the requirements for being saved are the same. As we become more equipped to live as saints of God our individual personalities emerge and we develop a character in Christ that is unique to us and to the place in the church that God has determined for each of us. The important thing is that our character is still based in the righteousness of God. When we make the decision to fill the place God has designated for each of us with a complete and total commitment according to God's will, we have made the decision to be perfect.

The important thing is that we walk after the Spirit and in obedience to the Word and the will of God. Let God be the Carpenter who carves the wood. Let God be the Potter who shapes the clay. You'll be amazed at the results!

If God can shape you so that you function perfectly, who says you can't do it?

5

THE PERFECT JOB

> There was a man in the land of Uz, whose name was
> Job; and that man was perfect and upright; and one that
> feared God and eschewed evil. Job 1:1

The book of Job opens by describing the character of a man.
The first thing we notice is that there is no reference to patience,
yet people often talk about the patience of Job. Where does that
come from?

> Take, my brethren, the prophets, who have spoken in the
> name of the Lord, for an example of suffering affliction,
> and of patience. Behold, we count them happy which
> endure. Ye have heard of the patience of Job, and have
> seen the end of the Lord; that the Lord is very pitiful,
> and of tender mercy. James 5:10-11

James was Bishop of the Jerusalem Church. The passage above
is an excerpt from his epistle to the Diaspora. Diaspora is the

name used to refer to the Jewish Christians who had scattered and were living outside the borders of Palestine. (Tenny 1976)

We know that these were Jews who had converted to Christianity because James, in the first verse, refers to them as "the twelve tribes which are scattered abroad." Whenever we see the term "twelve tribes" we know the reference is to the Children of Israel.

So, we know from the Scriptures that Job had patience, but patience does not produce perfection; patience is a by-product of perfection. That is a study for another time.

Let's take a closer look. The first verse in the book of Job reveals four aspects of Job's character.

1. Job was perfect.
2. Job was upright.
3. Job feared God.
4. Job eschewed evil.

The word "eschewed" comes from the Hebrew cuwr (pronounced soor). Translated it means:

- To go
- To take off
- To turn aside, avoid
- To be removed
- To take away
- To put away, depose, put aside
- To leave undone
- To retract, reject, abolish

In other words, Job avoided and rejected anything (thought, word, or deed) that was hurtful, harmful, or wicked.

The Scripture first states that Job was perfect. In order to understand what that means we need to go back to the original language. Perfect, in this passage, is translated from the Hebrew adjective "tam" (pronounced tawm). The word has a number of applications. We'll look at some Scriptures to help us understand the definitions. That's a good way to learn Bible principles, by the way. Compare Scriptures with Scriptures. God will always back up His own Word.

Undefiled—In the Old Testament to be undefiled means to be without blemish, without spot.

Blessed are the undefiled in the way, who walk in the law of the Lord. Psalm 119:1

The implication here is that a person who is undefiled is one who walks in the law of the Lord. In the Old Testament that would have been a reference to the Old Testament Law. But what does the Old Testament law represent, but the will of God? Therefore, to be unblemished in your way means you walk in the will of God.

Pure religion and undefiled before God and the Father is this, To visit the fatherless and widows in their affliction, and to keep himself unspotted from the world. James 1:27

In this passage, the word religion refers to ceremonial observance and worshipping. The attitude of a person whose worship and observance before God is pure and unblemished is reflected in their care for those in need. That type of person doesn't let the ways of the world (those thoughts, attitudes, and behavior that resist God) take up residence.

Upright

The righteous shall be glad in the Lord, and shall trust in him; and all the upright in heart shall glory. Psalm 64:10

The word upright literally means "straight." To understand this, think about the word "crooked." When something is crooked, it bends and twists and turns. When people are honest with you they speak in a straightforward manner. When people are sincere, they can look you straight in the eye. This passage talks about the upright heart, the heart that is clear and straight and sincere and honest.

Complete

For in him dwelleth all the fulness of the Godhead bodily. And ye are complete in him, which is the head of all principality and power:

Colossians 2:9-10

The word translated here that best fits is "replete." It means to be provided for in an abundant manner. God provides what we need. Sometimes it may not seem so, but we have to know the difference between needs and wants. And we have to understand that people don't always obey the Lord. Sometimes He will speak to people and send them to us to bless us, but those people won't always go.

I can remember times when I've been in need and God sent people to help. I can also remember times I've been in need; God sent people to help, and they refused to come. In all these things, I had to keep my faith completely in the Lord. Don't ever think God has forgotten you.

Being provided for doesn't just mean the natural things, though that always seems to be the first thing we think of.

Jesus said: The thief cometh not, but for to steal, and to kill, and to destroy: I am come that they might have life, and that they might have it more abundantly. John 10:10

That "abundant life" that we have in Jesus is a life that's much more than the day-to-day survival existence that we're used to. It's a life of victory and joy and peace. It's a heightened state of existence that helps us to rise above the cares of the world. The Bible calls it being "more than a conqueror." There will be cares and trouble and tribulation. I wonder sometimes about the fact that people will be joyfully saved, but the minute trouble strikes, the first thing out of their mouths is "Why me?" "Why did God let this happen to me?" But the Bible has never promised us a trouble free life. The Christian walk is not a walk where we are sanitized from everything that could go wrong. This world is under a curse. We are in this world; just not a part of it. But it is a more abundant life where we are sustained in the spirit and are not defeated by things that go wrong in our little universe.

Sound

Let my heart be sound in thy statutes; that I be not ashamed. Psalm 119:80

This translation of "sound" means entire. The heart must be entirely based in the statutes of God. This was the mistake Solomon made. His heart was not sound in God. There were flaws and gaps in his faith and it caused him to fail.

For God hath not given us the spirit of fear; but of power, and of love, and of a sound mind. 2 Timothy 1:7

Here the word "sound" translate means discipline and self control. Another word for this is temperance, which is a fruit of the Spirit. When we get to the point where we are yielded to God, temperance, that discipline, that self control that comes from the presence of His Spirit, gives us power over the flesh. God gives us the ability to control our thoughts and not let just anything take over our minds. We can discipline ourselves to reject ungodly things that Satan tries to put into our minds. When we're based in God, we can control ourselves against doing things that we know are ungodly, unhealthy, unsound, etc.

Wholesome

A wholesome tongue is a tree of life: but perverseness therein is a breach in the spirit. Proverbs 15:4

This is a good thing for every Christian to have. A wholesome tongue speaks words that have a healing rather than a destructive effect. Even when words of rebuke or correction are spoken, they have the effect of turning a person in the right direction.

Morally innocent

I am clean without transgression, I am innocent; neither is there iniquity in me. Job 33:9

In the Old Testament, it was very common to repeat a phrase several times but say it differently each time for clarification. Job said that he was without transgression (meaning he had done nothing wrong), that he was innocent (clear of any wrong) and that there was no iniquity in him (existing in a state or condition of innocence).

This is an interesting thought about the whole concept of the need for salvation through Jesus Christ. A person can be innocent and without transgression, but still not be saved because of the iniquity that exists within the soul. We are born into sin; therefore, regardless of how innocently we live and regardless of whether we never commit a wrong act against anyone, we still have the stain of original sin on our souls; we still exist in the condition of iniquity. Iniquity is the condition that gives us the potential to commit sin, like a gene that gives the potential for a certain hair color.

To be innocent in God's eyes means that He has cleansed us from all three of these things. We have a brand new start on life, cleared of past transgressions, innocent of wrongdoing, and cleansed from the iniquity of original sin.

Be careful. You can be morally innocent and still not be righteous before the Lord. Make sure you find out what God means by morally innocent rather than seeking to conform to the morality of the world. What is morally right in the world does not necessarily meet God's moral standard. Morality, by worldly standards, is often based on convenience, practicality, situations, emotion and profitability. What is right in one situation may be the right thing to do in another, depending on the variables. But what is wrong in one situation may be the right thing to do in another, again depending on the variables in the situation.

For example, in most societies a lie is considered unethical and the wrong thing to do. Yet in certain situations people will not hesitate to tell a lie, whether it be a serious one or what is called "a little white lie." By the standards of the world, a lie becomes a covenient action and the circumstances change the nature of the offense from wrong to convenient or expedient.

By God's standards it is a lie, nonetheless. The Word of God says that all liars are unrighteous.

> But the fearful, and unbelieving, and the abominable, and murderers, and whoremongers, and sorcerers, and

idolaters, and all liars, shall have their part in the lake which burneth with fire and brimstone: which is the second death. Revelation 21:8

Does that seem extreme? Consider the principle behind the practice.

Ye are of your father the devil, and the lusts of your father ye will do. He was a murderer from the beginning, and abode not in the truth, because there is no truth in him. When he speaketh a lie, he speaketh of his own: for he is a liar, and the father of it. John 8:44

Satan is a liar and the father of lies. He gives birth to them. He will try to trick you into thinking that "little white lie" you told wasn't really a lie or wrong, but a simple act of expediency. Remember that he is the prince of this world and will try to lead you to live by wordly attitudes because he knows they will lead you away from God.

The truth of the matter is this. A lie is a deliberate attempt to mask or evade the truth and to deceive the listener. That's not the character of God; it's the character of Satan, and that's why the telling of a lie has such serious implications.

God acknowledged Job as perfect:

And the LORD said unto Satan, Hast thou considered my servant Job, that there is none like him in the earth, a perfect and an upright man, one that feareth God, and escheweth evil? Job 1:8

The question is this. If God acknowledged Job to be perfect, and perfect refers to the qualities of character we have just discussed, what is there in these qualities we cannot achieve with the help of the Lord? With all the backup, support, and help that God has given and continues to give us, who says we can't:

- Be Undefiled?
- Live Upright?
- Be Complete?
- Be Sound?
- Be Wholesome?
- Be Morally Innocent?
- Have integrity?
- Be Morally and Ethically Pure?

God commands it so it must be possible. If God says we can do it; if God says we can be perfect, who says we can't?

6

THE IMPERFECT SOLOMON

Solomon, the third king to rule in Israel, was the tenth son of David, the second king of that nation.

David fathered six sons while he was living in Hebron: Amnon, Chileab, Absalom, Adonijah, Shepatiah, and Ithream (Second Samuel 3:2-5). While he was living in Jerusalem David fathered Shammuah, Shobab, Nathan, Solomon, Ibhar, Elishua, Nepheg, Japhia, Elishama, Eliada, and Eliphalet (Second Samuel 5:14-16).

Solomon was the second son of Bathsheba, the first having been taken by the Lord as punishment for David's sin. When he was born, the Lord loved Solomon and sent Nathan the prophet to give him a second name, Jedidiah, which meant "beloved of the Lord."

> And David comforted Bathsheba his wife, and went in unto her, and lay with her: and she bare a son, and he called his name Solomon: and the LORD loved him.

And he sent by the hand of Nathan the prophet; and he
called his name Jedidiah, because of the LORD. 2 Samuel
12:24-25

Financially speaking, Solomon never knew a day's worry. He
never knew hunger or poverty. There were no cold nights in the
hills with the flocks as his father had known. Solomon never
had to fight for his life or wage war against anyone. He was a
pampered child, yet he did know something about the darker
side of life.

Before he grew to maturity several of his older half
brothers had met violent deaths and one-half sister had
been raped. (Tenny, 1976, 470)

Solomon's childhood was spent in the midst of unrest, violence,
and intrigue. He saw his brothers try to dethrone his father and
even saw his father take to the hills to escape the treachery of
his half-brother Absalom.

Solomon was not the eldest son but he was to receive the promise
from God to rule:

Behold, a son shall be born to thee, who shall be a man
of rest; and I will give him rest from all his enemies round
about: for his name shall be Solomon, and I will give peace
and quietness unto Israel in his days. 1 Chronicles 22:9

The time came for Solomon to ascend to the throne and it
seemed as if the fulfillment of God's promise was threatened.
Solomon's half-brother Adonijah attempted to take the throne,

first by trying to have himself anointed king, and secondly, by trying to trick Solomon into giving him Abishag, David's concubine. In that era, the king's concubines were usually passed on to the next king after the current ruler died. Had Solomon made the error of giving Abishag to Adonijah, it would have been equivalent to acknowledging Adonijah as the next potential ruler. Solomon defended his throne by having Adonijah and Joab executed and Abiathar exiled. He placed Shimei under city arrest with the threat of death if he set foot out of Jerusalem. Shimei later violated that injunction and lost his life.

Solomon's brothers protested his ascension to the throne, but I believe the people were in favor of it, mainly because of David. For one thing, the rule of succession had not yet been firmly established. Any claim Adonijah made to the throne would have had to compete with the choice of David. That was a major factor because the people loved David. In 2 Samuel 3:36 the Scripture tells us that whatever David did pleased all the people. His soldiers called him "the light of Israel" (2 Samuel 21:14). The people counted David as being worth "ten thousand" of themselves (2 Samuel 18:3). I believe they would have followed anyone David chose to put on the throne after himself.

David commented on Solomon's youth and inexperience (1 Chronicles 29:1), which indicates that Solomon may not have been trained in the finer points of leadership, and probably wasn't ready for the task. Adonijah forced David's hand by trying to usurp the throne. Solomon himself did not feel capable of ruling the nation. He readily admitted to God that he was a child, not knowing how to go out or come in. He did look to God for guidance, at least in the early days of his reign. Solomon was young, scared, inexperienced, and faced with the rule of a huge kingdom without and treachery from within. I believe at that moment, he would have agreed to anything God said.

Solomon enjoyed two advantages when he took the throne. First, God had promised him protection and peace in Israel all the days of his rule. That eliminated issues which would be a major concern of any ruler. Solomon was not a man of war, nor did he need to be. Second, Solomon was in the favorable position of having been chosen for rule by Israel's beloved shepherd king. His popularity with the people was guaranteed.

As he ruled Israel, the gift of wisdom that God had promised him began to reveal itself in Solomon. People came from everywhere to hear him speak. Scripture says that he spoke 3,000 proverbs and 1,005 songs. God also fulfilled his promise of riches and honor. Solomon was wealthier than any king before him had ever been.

Four years after he took the throne, Solomon entered into a period of construction. He levied taxes, drafted men, and enlisted the help of Hiram of Tyre to build the temple of the Lord. Solomon completed the temple in seven years. The dedication ceremony was replete with many sacrifices, great ceremony, and Solomon's prayer wherein he entreated the Lord for mercy and grace upon Israel. Thirteen years later Solomon completed his own house sparing no expense and no labor.

Solomon was fervent in prayer and in the promises he made to God, yet it seemed he was of two minds. Although he seemed to be honoring the statues of David his father, and seemed to love the Lord, he sacrificed and burnt incense in high places. Events came to pass that revealed his true priorities.

Almost immediately after ascending to the throne, Solomon broke the holy law. He entered into a treaty with pharaoh and married pharaoh's daughter.

> "It was common practice in those days to make political alliances with surrounding nations by intermarriage among the royal families" (Rogers 2005)

In Solomon's case, however, God's promise made political marriages unnecessary. Intermarriage with the pagan nations was also a violation of the commandment of the Lord. The fact that these marriages happened is a commentary not only on Solomon's lack of faith but also on his character. Even if he needed to marry to secure the nation's borders, he was not surrounded by 700 countries! But Solomon had 700 wives, as well as 300 concubines. In his 40 years of rule, with 700 wives, that meant Solomon would have had to get married every 21 days! Not only did he display instability of character, but he was a man who lacked control, a person of excess.

> But although Solomon was become the most glorious of kings, and the best beloved by God, and had exceeded in wisdom and riches those that had been rulers of the Hebrews before him, yet did not he persevere in this happy state till he died. Nay, he forsook the observation of the laws of his fathers, and came to an end no way suitable to our foregoing history of him. He grew mad

in his love of women, and laid no restraint on himself in his lusts; nor was he satisfied with the women of his country alone, but he married many wives out of foreign nations; Sidonians, and Tyrians, and Ammonites, and Edomites; and he transgressed the laws of Moses, which forbade Jews to marry any but those that were of their own people. (Josephus 1987)

Solomon was not completely committed to the statutes of God and his heart was not perfect before the Lord. His ambivalent attitude toward God was rooted in a double mind that caused him to walk a double road. Even as he was building the temple and making prayer to God, Solomon broke the holy law and began to marry strange women. His first wrong marriage was to the daughter of the Egyptian Pharaoh. He knew that he was wrong in doing so. He even had a separate house built for her because the house of David was holy and he didn't want her to live in it.

And Solomon brought up the daughter of Pharaoh out of the city of David unto the house that he had built for her: for he said, My wife shall not dwell in the house of David king of Israel, because the places are holy, whereunto the ark of the LORD hath come. 2 Chronicles 8:11

The double-minded king was trying to lead a double life. It seemed acceptable to fraternize with pagans and fellowship with God, as long as they were kept separate. How many Christians today profess God in one place (the church) and serve the world, the flesh, and the devil in another? That's definitely not the behavior of a perfect heart.

Solomon had stepped onto the slippery slope. His downward spiral had begun. His apostasy was not a sudden thing. It started with an imperfect, partially committed heart and uncontrolled inordinate desires. These weaknesses were the vehicle through which his strange wives turned his heart from God. The lust that was already in Solomon's heart was the tool Satan used to bring him down. We can never say that the sins of others caused us to fall. That's equivalent to saying that God cannot keep us if we want to be kept. If we are truly and wholly committed to the Lord, then nothing can separate us from the love of Christ. Blaming others, as well following others into sin, is an excuse and an attempt to cover the sin that is within our heart.

As is the case with any addiction, Solomon's habit became his master.

> He also began to worship their gods, which he did in order to the gratification of his wives, and out of his affection for them. This very thing our legislator suspected, and so admonished us beforehand, that we should not marry women of other countries, lest we should be entangled with foreign customs, and apostatize from our own; lest we should leave off to honor our own God, and should worship their gods. But Solomon was Gllen (sic) headlong into unreasonable pleasures, and regarded not those admonitions; for when he had married seven hundred wives, the daughters of princes and of eminent persons, and three hundred concubines, and those besides the king of Egypt's daughter, he soon was governed by them, till he came to imitate their practices. He was forced to give them this demonstration of his

kindness and affection to them, to live according to the laws of their countries. And as he grew into years, and his reason became weaker by length of time, it was not sufficient to recall to his mind the institutions of his own country; so he still more and more contemned his own God, and continued to regard the gods that his marriages had introduced nay, before this happened, he sinned, and fell into an error about the observation of the laws, when he made the images of brazen oxen that supported the brazen sea, and the images of lions about his own throne; for these he made, although it was not agreeable to piety so to do; and this he did, notwithstanding that he had his father as a most excellent and domestic pattern of virtue, and knew what a glorious character he had left behind him, because of his piety towards God. Nor did he imitate David, although God had twice appeared to him in his sleep, and exhorted him to imitate his father. (Josephus 1987)

God had already twice warned Solomon about the consequences of disobedience. Solomon had used up his bonus card. All the holes were punched. The Lord sent the prophet Ahijah to pronounce the final judgment. All the glory of the cities Solomon built, the gardens, the pools, the art, the wealth, and the words of wisdom could not erase his sin. Solomon was laid to rest with his fathers before him, leaving a legacy of apostasy for which others would have to suffer. Solomon's transgression was visited upon his son and Israel was cut off from the land just as God had promised. The kingdom was split and ten tribes were given to Solomon's chief overseer Jeroboam. The Lord allowed the other two tribes (Benjamin and Judah) to stay under

Rehoboam's rule. He did this for David's sake, because He had promised David that he would forever have a light on the throne.

King Solomon was of a very different character than his father David. Where David was a warrior, Solomon was a man of peace. David grew up in hardship and leanness, whereas Solomon never suffered want for anything. Wealth is not necessarily a disadvantage or a shortcoming. The key is in the use of it.

Based on what the Scriptures tell us, we see that Solomon lived an indulgent and excessive lifestyle. He overtaxed his subjects when he could have used his royal funds for the purposes he entertained. Solomon's taxation approach and his practice of forcing the people into government labor showed little concern for the well being of his subjects. David had a perfect heart before God. He was humble, submitted to God, quick to repent when he had sinned, but Solomon showed no such tendencies until he was near the end of his life.

A reading of Solomon's dedication prayer at the temple reveals a curious thing. All through the prayer there are phrases such as "forgive the sin of thy servants," and "judge thy servants," and "that they may fear thee," and "if they sin against thee." The only time Solomon actually includes himself in the prayer is to lay claim to his own accomplishment, to say that he built the Lord's house (1 Kings 8:20, 27, 43, 44, 48). It's as if Solomon felt by building the temple he had fulfilled his requirement to serve God and therefore could distance himself from any further involvement or requirement to serve. It seemed it was now up to the people to be loyal to the Lord. Solomon even admonished them to walk perfect before God, even though he had not done so in his own life.

> And it was so, that when Solomon had made an end of praying all this prayer and supplication unto the LORD, he arose from before the altar of the LORD, from kneeling on his knees with his hands spread up to heaven. And he stood, and blessed all the congregation of Israel with a loud voice, saying, Blessed be the LORD, that hath given rest unto his people Israel, according to all that he promised: there hath not failed one word of all his good promise, which he promised by the hand of Moses his servant. The LORD our God be with us, as he was with our fathers: let him not leave us, nor forsake us: That he may incline our hearts unto him, to walk in all his ways, and to keep his commandments, and his statutes, and his judgments, which he commanded our fathers. And let these my words, wherewith I have made supplication before the LORD, be nigh unto the LORD our God day and night, that he maintain the cause of his servant, and the cause of his people Israel at all times, as the matter shall require: That all the people of the earth may know that the LORD is God, and that there is none else. Let your heart therefore be perfect with the LORD our God, to walk in his statutes, and to keep his commandments, as at this day. 1 Kings 8:54-61

David's prayers, in contrast, demonstrated a perfect heart before God and a personal acceptance of his responsibility to God. David prayed in the first person, holding himself accountable to God as a man and as a leader. Solomon prayed in the third person, holding the people of Israel accountable. Later in life, as indicated in the Book of Ecclesiastes, Solomon seems to have finally discovered the right perspective. The Book starts out with bitter statements about the uselessness of wisdom. That's what happens when we lose sight of God. Life seems meaningless and useful, and despair is often the order of the day.

God gave Solomon the gift of wisdom so he could rightly judge the people. But he began to lean to his own understanding. Solomon began to see wisdom as an end in itself instead of a means to a godly end. Solomon frequently quotes himself as having sought and acquired much wisdom, as though God had not bestowed the gift upon him. He focused more on the gift than on the Gift Giver. Solomon internalized the gift so much that he began to see himself as its source. God gave the gift but Solomon used it without any further guidance from the Lord. How often do we get proud in the fact that God is using us and begin to see ourselves as the source of people's blessings?

Solomon indulged himself to the exclusion of his Creator and thereby lost the value and meaning of life as it is meant to be. Too late, he realized that life has no significance without God.

It all happened because Solomon's commitment to God was lacking and his heart was not perfect with God.

> For it came to pass, when Solomon was old, that his wives turned away his heart after other gods: and his heart was not perfect with the LORD his God, as was the heart of David his father. For Solomon went after Ashtoreth the goddess of the Zidonians, and after Milcom the

abomination of the Ammonites. And Solomon did evil in the sight of the LORD, and went not fully after the LORD, as did David his father. 1 Kings 11:4-6

Solomon made two serious errors that brought about his downfall:

1. His heart was not perfect with God.
2. Because his heart was not perfect with God, he didn't seek the Lord in a complete manner.

The word translated to perfect in this passage is "shalam" meaning complete, full and peaceable. Solomon was not at complete peace in his relationship with God, nor did he seek God in a completely dedicated manner.

So we have a tragic example of how not to be perfect. There are many lessons we can take from this sad situation:

Be real and complete in your commitment to God.

> And thou shalt love the Lord thy God with all thy heart, and with all thy soul, and with all thy mind, and with all thy strength: this is the first commandment. Mark 12:30

Be focused and disciplined in your Christian life.

> I therefore so run, not as uncertainly; so fight I, not as one that beateth the air: But I keep under my body, and bring it into subjection: lest that by any means, when I have preached to others, I myself should be a castaway. 1 Corinthians 9:26-27

Don't be double-minded. Either you believe God or you don't.

> For he that wavereth is like a wave of the sea driven with the wind and tossed. For let not that man think that he shall receive any thing of the Lord. A double minded man is unstable in all his ways. James 1:6-8

Check yourself, especially when correcting someone else.

> Brethren, if a man be overtaken in a fault, ye which are spiritual, restore such an one in the spirit of meekness; considering thyself, lest thou also be tempted.
> Galatians 6:1

Either you walk after the Spirit or after the flesh. You can't do both.

> This I say then, Walk in the Spirit, and ye shall not fulfil the lust of the flesh. Galatians 5:16

It is a common error to rejoice when we encounter someone in the Bible who is as flawed and has some of the same shortcomings we have. We should remember that some situations and narratives are not in the Bible to make us feel good about ourselves. It's not appropriate to dwell on how good we think we are compared to how badly we think others behave. It's not appropriate to feel okay about the sins we commit just because we find that someone else has committed those same sins. That doesn't make it all right. These examples are there for our teaching and admonition, so that we don't go down the same path.

As we consider the imperfect condition of Solomon's heart and mind, we should be forewarned of the path we may find ourselves on if we are not fully committed to serving God and following the way He has laid out for us.

Solomon's heart was not perfect, but yours can be!

7

NOAH—PERFECT
IN HIS GENERATIONS

The man Noah was a pivot point between two eras. The generations of man before Noah were the descendants of Adam and Eve. Their behavior was the result of humankind's fall from grace.

> And God saw that the wickedness of man was great in the earth, and that every imagination of the thoughts of his heart was only evil continually. Genesis 6:5

All the good things God had created had become corrupted by sin. The Lord God determined that there was no way to fix it; the inhabitants of the earth were ruined. They had to be removed.

On a side note, think about the new birth. We who are corrupted by sin cannot be changed, because we are ruined. The seed of corruption is within the man of flesh who was "conceived in sin and shaped in iniquity."

> Behold, I was shapen in iniquity, and in sin did my mother conceive me. Psalm 51:5

We are conceived in sin because we are conceived in the flesh and no good thing abides in the flesh. It is corrupt in sin. That's why we have to be born again. The man of flesh has been ruined by sin and must die; the man of the spirit has to be born in us so that we are capable to receive the will of God and live by it. The incidents that occurred between God and Noah can be seen as a type of the cycle of salvation; that is, the death of the man of flesh and the birth of the new man raised in righteousness and true holiness.

> But ye have not so learned Christ; If so be that ye have heard him, and have been taught by him, as the truth is in Jesus: That ye put off concerning the former conversation the old man, which is corrupt according to the deceitful lusts; And be renewed in the spirit of your mind; And that ye put on the new man, which after God is created in righteousness and true holiness. Ephesians 4:20-24

The basic result of walking in the will of God is that there must be a distinct difference between the people of God and the people who are not of God. Note the Scripture:

> And God saw that the wickedness of man was great in the earth, and that every imagination of the thoughts of his heart was only evil continually. And it repented the

LORD that he had made man on the earth, and it grieved him at his heart. Genesis 6:5-6

God saw the wickedness and continual evil imaginations of man that were a reflection of humankind being corrupted by sin. And He made a comparison between Noah and the generations of people that walked the earth at that time.

But Noah found grace in the eyes of the LORD. These are the generations of Noah: Noah was a just man and perfect in his generations, and Noah walked with God. Genesis 6:8-9

The Scripture mentions three characteristics that caused Noah to find grace in the eyes of the Lord:

1. Noah was a just man.
2. Noah was perfect in his generations.
3. Noah walked with God.

The word translated "just" in this passage is "tsaddiyq" pronounced (tsad deek). It means just and righteous. When we act in a just manner we do what is right naturally, morally and legally, according to the will of God.

How does one know to do right naturally? I used to believe that when God created man and breathed life into him, He left a trace of His Spirit as man's guide to righteousness. That's a pretty sentiment, but it's not correct. We must be careful not to make the mistake of having a sentimental point of view regarding God. Sentiment is based on emotion and emotion is rooted in the heart. The Bible tells us that the heart is deceitful. When we paint a portrait of God based on feelings instead of on Scripture, our heart will give us a god that makes it feel good about itself without having to do any self-examination or make any adjustments. Our heart will manufacture a god that is recreated after its own image, a god that says we're okay in our current condition. That's not the God of Scripture.

How does the heart recreate God in its own image? It reduces God to a god with which it can be comfortable at the emotional level without having to make any changes in itself. We basically see Him as being equal with us, co-existent, one may say. That reduces the God of the Bible to the level of the created, rather than recognizing Him on His level as the Creator. The heart (the carnal man) attempts to remove all need for change and/or regeneration by saying that God is everywhere, in everything, in us, and is the same as us. Ergo, we are already like Him and He is already like us! So everybody is just fine! That's not correct and it's not Scripture. To begin with, God does not automatically live in everybody and everything. He exists above and apart from that which He has created, even man. We see God's handiwork in everything He has created, for it all reflects His glory. It is as if we're witnessing the skill and gifts and capabilities of the Master Craftsman through seeing those things He has created. When God created man He created him in His own image, thereby giving him life and thought and free will.

God does not live in everybody. The Scripture is clear on this. We must meet certain conditions for God's Spirit to live in us.

And Jesus answered and said unto him, "If a man love me, he will keep my words, and my Father will love him, and we will come down unto him, and make our abode with him." John 14:23 KJV

And we are his witnesses of these things; and so is also the Holy Ghost, whom God hath given to them that obey him. Acts 5:32 KJV

It seems as if one Scripture in the book of Ephesians does say that God is in everyone:

There is one body, and one Spirit, even as ye are called in one hope of your calling; One Lord, one faith, one baptism, One God and Father of all, who is above all, and through all, and in you all. Ephesians 4:5-6 KJV

This passage seems to say that God lives in everyone, but upon closer examination, we understand that it doesn't say that at all. Paul is speaking to the Christians at the church in Ephesus, not to unbelievers. Paul speaks of faith. Who would have faith in God but a believer? Paul speaks of baptism. Who would be baptized but a believer? Paul is confirming that believers become one in the Spirit of God, because they all share submission to the Lord, faith in the Lord, baptism in the faith and the grace of Christ. Believers are one in the Lord, because they are united by the common indwelling of God, the Holy Spirit. He is the One who makes us a community of believers, united in the faith as one to form the body of Christ.

In addition we know that God does not abide in everyone because His Spirit will not dwell in unholy places. Paul stressed this fact to the Church at Corinth:

> Know ye not that ye are the temple of God, and that the Spirit of God dwelleth in you? If any man defile the temple of God, him shall god destroy; for the temple of God is holy, which temple you are. 1 Corinthians 3:16-17 KJV

This is further proof that God does not dwell in everyone, because God recognizes as holy only believers who have been born again of the water and the Spirit.

Noah was a believer but he hadn't received the promise— conversion and the new birth, followed by the indwelling of God's Spirit. How, then, did he know the right thing to do? We're back to the original question . . . how does one know naturally to do the right thing? The Jews had the law that was teaching them right from wrong, but the Gentiles had something else to go by:

> For when the Gentiles, which have not the law, do by nature the things contained in the law, these, having not the law, are a law unto themselves; which show the work of the law written in their hearts, their conscience also bearing witness, and their thoughts the mean while accusing or else excusing one another . . . Romans 2:14-15 KJV

How did the Gentiles acquire a nature that showed them right and wrong? Where did that conscience come from? The key word here is "nature." When Adam and Eve ate of the forbidden fruit they were separated from God spiritually and had to live by their own nature, by natural means.

Adam's sin spiritually separated the human race from its Creator. Adam's sin also planted a seed into man's spiritual makeup. They ate the fruit from the tree of the knowledge of good and evil. They became implanted with the knowledge of good and evil, of right and wrong. That knowledge manifested itself immediately, because they instantly felt the shame of their disobedience. They weren't necessarily ashamed of their nakedness. They were exposed in their sinfulness and covered up in the only way they knew how. But still they knew the voice of God when they heard it. There is nowhere in Scripture that tells us man forgot the sound of the voice of God or didn't know when God when speaking to him.

We, the human race, are descendents of Adam. As such, we inherited the guilt of Adam's transgression as well as the capability for sin, like a bad genetic code. We also inherited Adam's nature. Embedded in that nature is the result of his transgression. The knowledge of good and evil that Adam received from eating of the forbidden tree was passed down to us, his descendents. We carry within us the knowledge of good and evil, of right and wrong. That's the conscience of which the Scripture speaks in the second chapter of the book of Romans.

That brings us to Noah. Noah, like all mankind, was imprinted with the knowledge of good and evil, of right and wrong. And Noah was a just man, perfect in his generations. He always chose what was good and right, and always avoided what was evil and wrong. He knew the difference because the knowledge was in him; it was written in his heart. He knew the voice of God because the knowledge of that voice was still with man.

Noah was perfect in his generations. The generations are the times during which a person lives. Noah was sincere in his behavior and without blemish. He was clear of the sin that abounded in his time and behaved righteously during a time when everyone else was behaving wrongly. In his generation, the people were behaving wickedly and were sunk in sin. Noah refused to sink into that pit. He insisted on doing what he knew to be the right thing. He insisted on living a righteous life before God.

Noah walked with God. Let's go back a bit in the Scripture to the Garden of Eden:

> And they heard the voice of the LORD God walking in the garden in the cool of the day: and Adam and his wife hid themselves from the presence of the LORD God amongst the trees of the garden. Genesis 3:8 KJV

When first created, Adam and Eve apparently met God as He walked in the garden. After their sin, instead of meeting Him they hid from Him.

The implication is that Noah was conversant with God. He interacted with Him and behaved according to God's expressed requirements. Are you conversant with God? You can be. Everyone can be. The prophet Isaiah says, "Seek ye the Lord while He may be found. Call upon him while he is near." (Isaiah 55:6) Jesus was conversant with the Father. He prayed all the time. The Bible admonishes us to pray without ceasing.

When God spoke to Noah and commanded him to build the ark, Noah obeyed the will of God, as was already his way.

> Thus did Noah; according to all that God commanded him, so did he. Genesis 6:22 KJV

The Scripture tells us that Noah did all that the Lord commanded him to do. The flood came and was upon the earth 40 days and 40 nights, after which time the ark came to rest on Mount Ararat and the floods were dried from the land. There was no one left alive but Noah and his family.

When Noah left the ark, he did run into a bit of trouble. He planted a vineyard, drank of his own wine and got drunk and lay naked in his tent. This is what the Bible means when it says:

> Wine is a mocker, strong drink is raging: and whosoever is deceived thereby is not wise. Proverbs 20:1 KJV

Too much wine will make a fool out of a person and strong drink is raging (that means strong liquor will make you stupid and loud and coarse and strange and many other negative things that happen to people when they've had too much to drink).

Noah's sons had enough respect that they went in and covered him. The Bible doesn't say that drinking is a sin, but one has to wonder . . . how does it glorify God considering what it does to a person and how it makes a person behave? There are many things that may not be sin but can evolve into or cause sinful acts. The Bible calls them weights.

> Wherefore seeing we also are compassed about with so great a cloud of witnesses, let us lay aside every weight, and the sin which doth so easily beset us, and let us run with patience the race that is set before us, Hebrews 12:1 KJV

In this context, a weight is something that can be a burden or a hindrance. That's why some things, even though they may not be sinful in themselves, need to be laid aside, because they can hinder us and keep us from reaching the right place in God.

Anyway, the main point of this chapter is that Noah obeyed God and through him humankind got a new start, because only eight people survived the flood—Noah, his wife, his three sons, and their wives. That was the seed for the new population of the earth. God said the same thing to Noah that He had said to Adam and Eve. Just as He had commanded Adam and Eve to be fruitful and multiply and replenish the earth, so He commanded Noah and his family:

> And God blessed Noah and his sons, and said unto them, Be fruitful, and multiply, and replenish the earth. Genesis 9:1 KJV

Because of Noah, the human race had another chance.

The Scripture says that Noah was "perfect in his generations." That means Noah was without fault in his intention to please God, and that he strived to live righteous in an unrighteous world, because his heart was committed to God. He refused to take part in the sin that was going on around him.

Can you be perfect in your generations? Can you let God help you to live righteous in an unrighteous world? Will you refuse to take part in the sin that's happening around you? God has given you the power to do that. God believes you can do that. If God believes you can be perfect, who is anyone to say that you can't?

BIBLIOGRAPHY

Ambridge, Reverend L.N. *A Word of Hope, Revised Edition.* Bloomington: XLibris, 2011.

Josephus. *The Works of Josephus: New Updated Edition.* Peabody: Hendrickson Publishers, Inc., 1987.

Rogers, Thomas R., D.Min. *The Panorama of the Old Testament.* Newburgh: Trinity Press, 2005.

Tenny, Merril C., ed. *Zondervan Pictorial Encyclopaedia of the Bible.* Vol. 5. 5 vols. Grand Rapids, Michigan: Regency Reference Library, 1976.